MORE Mother's Thoughts for the Day

MORE Mother's Thoughts for the Day

TWENTY-FIVE YEARS OF WISDOM

COMPILED BY M.C. Sungaila

Crystal Cove
PRESS

Copyright © 2020 M.C. Sungaila

All rights reserved.

No part of this book may be reproduced, or stored in a retrieval system, or transmitted in any form or by any means, electronic, mechanical, photocopying, recording, or otherwise, without express written permission of the publisher.

Disclaimer: Note that this book includes quotations that originally appeared in public domain sources or that are briefly excerpted from longer works.

Published by Crystal Cove Press, Newport Beach, California
www.mothersthoughtsfortheday.com

Edited and designed by Girl Friday Productions
www.girlfridayproductions.com
Design: Paul Barrett
Project management: Katherine Richards

ISBN (hardcover): 978-1-7338657-2-2
ISBN (paperback): 978-1-7338657-3-9
LCCN: 2020906703

First edition

PREFACE

From the time I was in college, my mother has sent me bite-size insights, reassurances, and pieces of wisdom on a daily basis, in handwritten letters and later by text message. Whether sent by letter or text, her words were always just what I needed to hear at precisely the right time.

Many of these bits of wisdom were collected in the first volume of *Mother's Thoughts for the Day*. Readers of that volume have shared it with their children, from grade school to college age. Others keep the volume on their desks, to refer to when they face challenges at work.

We hope this volume will provide similar encouragement, and warmth, to more people and families.

Enjoy!

M.C. Sungaila

Mother's thought for the day

Today is the tomorrow you worried about yesterday.

Love,
Mother

MORE Mother's Thoughts for the Day

NEVER LET ANYBODY TELL YOU THAT YOU

can't.

WINNERS

get ahead of **EVERYTHING.**

You know what you have to do.

You go, girl!

You need to let things go and MOVE ON.

Otherwise, you will stay stuck on the ground and you will NEVER FLY.

DO NOT LET A

challenge

BECOME AN EXCUSE FOR

not doing something.

You cannot control the **CHALLENGES** you encounter,

ONLY HOW YOU *respond* TO THEM.

Figure out a way to get it

DONE.

SOMETIMES YOU HAVE TO *be better* THAN EVERYONE ELSE.

Just do it.

I'VE BEEN READING ABOUT
SOME OF OUR GREAT COACHES.

They all believe in excellence.

EXCELLENCE IS NOT ACHIEVED BY CHANGING RULES AND GOALS TO MATCH YOUR PRESENT SKILLS. INSTEAD, EXCELLENCE IS ACHIEVED BY BUILDING YOUR SKILLS TO ACHIEVE YOUR GOALS.

Not an *easy* thing to do.

SO MUCH EASIER TO MOVE THE GOALPOST CLOSER.

DON'T *downplay* WHAT YOU HAVE DONE,

OR YOUR

skill.

YOU MADE THIS OPPORTUNITY. IT WASN'T HANDED TO YOU. EMBRACE IT. ENJOY THE MOMENT. DON'T FORGET TO TAKE THE LORD'S HAND AND WALK IN THERE TOGETHER.

P.S.

MY SPIRIT WILL BE WITH YOU TOO.

I DON'T KNOW WHY, BUT I BELIEVE YOU WILL DO JUST FINE WITH THIS OPPORTUNITY. NOT SAYING YOU WILL WIN, BUT I THINK THAT AT LEAST (AT THE MINIMUM) YOU WILL ESTABLISH YOUR CREDENTIALS AS A PERSON OF *substance.*

A PERSON WHO CAN THINK AND FUNCTION *outside the box.*

NOT MANY PEOPLE DO, YOU KNOW.

GET NICE AND COZY WITH A WARM CUP OF

lemon water.

Love you. Have a nice sleep

AND A GOOD DAY WITH

friends.

WOW! THAT WAS A *TOUGH SITUATION* YOU HAD TO ENDURE TODAY. SHOULD NOT HAVE HAPPENED. IT WAS WRONG ON *SOOOO* MANY LEVELS.

YOU HANDLED IT WAY BETTER THAN I WOULD HAVE. NICE TO SEE YOU THINK ON YOUR FEET AND DO IT WITH **DIGNITY.**

It's ok to cry.

IT'S OK TO POUND THE FLOOR. FRUSTRATION IS NOT A FUN EMOTION. ONCE YOU ARE DONE HAVING YOUR ADULT MELTDOWN, *ask this question:* DID YOU DO THE VERY BEST YOU COULD DO? IF THE ANSWER IS YES, PICK YOURSELF UP OFF THE FLOOR AND MOVE ON.

Good days are not always about *winning the fight* so much as *keeping your dignity.* You can always win another day. You cannot get back your dignity.

What's important is that you learn something, and do your best. When you ask yourself, "Was that the very best I could do?" and your answer is "For that time, that day, I did my very best," that's a win, baby.

That's a win!!

TAKE DEEP BREATHS. LET EVERYTHING SETTLE DOWN AND GEL.

CENTER *yourself.*

LET THINGS FALL IN PLACE.

YOU ARE PREPARED. THE ANSWERS ARE FILED IN YOUR BRAIN. YOU WILL NEED TO CENTER YOURSELF SO THAT YOU CAN LOCATE THEM.

REMEMBER TO TAKE HIS HAND AS YOU WALK IN. IF YOU FORGET TO TAKE HIS HAND, DON'T WORRY. HE WILL BE THERE STANDING WITH YOU. HE'S GOT YOUR BACK, KID!

YOU GO, GIRL!

LET YOUR MIND SEE BEAUTY.

Be free.

LET YOUR MIND RELAX.

Take a walk **WITH YOUR BEST FRIEND.** Take another walk **WITH YOUR BEST FRIEND.**

If I had a daughter, I'd want her to be just like you.

WAIT A MINUTE!! YOU ARE MY DAUGHTER. YOU *ARE* MY DAUGHTER, MY FRIEND.

I am a lucky lady.

This is one of those times you did everything right, **AND YOU STILL DID NOT GET THE BRASS RING.**

THAT'S BECAUSE

the brass ring was moved!

ALWAYS DO AND BE THE *best* THAT YOU CAN.

IN OTHER WORDS, BE *you.*

TREAT THIS EXPERIENCE AS A LESSON, *not a loss.*

IT WILL ONLY BE A LOSS IF YOU DO NOT GAIN *knowledge.*

REMEMBER:

Life is falling; living is getting up—and **CHARGING** forward even when you don't want to.

SAW THIS TODAY:

"Be someone who makes you happy."

GOOD ADVICE.

Quote from Albert Einstein:

"IF A CLUTTERED DESK IS THE SIGN OF A CLUTTERED MIND, OF WHAT, THEN, IS AN EMPTY DESK A SIGN?"

I liked that one!

BILL BENNETT JUST SAID SOMETHING:

"Morality Is Timeless."

SIMPLE, VERY SIMPLE. *YES, MORALITY IS TIMELESS.* THERE IS NO DIFFERENCE BETWEEN BUSINESS MORALITY OR PERSONAL MORALITY. YOU EITHER ARE MORAL OR YOU ARE NOT.

Truth is simple. It's really not complex.

POW!

MEET THE DAY WITH GUSTO.

Make this the best day . . .

ever!

READING A LETTER FROM A PASTOR—THIS SENTENCE POPPED OUT AT ME:

"If you don't stand for something, you will fall for anything."

KIND OF SAYS IT ALL, DOESN'T IT!

JUST BE YOU.

You know what you want to say.

SHOWTIME!

Walk away from the table when things are *changed.*

STOP NEGOTIATING
when they move the goalpost!

FUN PLAYING

Scrabble.

LET'S DO IT AGAIN.
MAYBE I CAN USE
MORE THAN
three-letter words
NEXT TIME!

Ownership of what we do wrong is as important as taking ownership of what we do right.

We don't always win the trophy.

Love you.

There are people who **DO** and people who **WISH**

...and you're the captain of the *first*.

ABOUT THE AUTHOR

M.C. Sungaila lives and works in Orange County, California, where she grew up. Her mother does too.

www.ingramcontent.com/pod-product-compliance
Lightning Source LLC
Chambersburg PA
CBHW061151070526
44584CB00034B/4479